LAWNS

The Gardener's Collection

Better Homes and Gardens® Books

Des Moines

MEREDITH® BOOKS
President, Book Group: Joseph J. Ward
Vice President and Editorial Director: Elizabeth P. Rice
Art Director: Ernest Shelton

LAWNS
Senior Editor: Marsha Jahns
Editor: Sharon Novotne O'Keefe
Art Director: Michael Burns
Copy Editors: Durrae Johanek, Kay Sanders, David Walsh
Assistant Editor: Jennifer Weir
Administrative Assistant: Carla Horner
Special thanks: Monica Brandies

MEREDITH CORPORATION CORPORATE OFFICERS:
Chairman of the Executive Committee: E. T. Meredith III
**Chairman of the Board, President
and Chief Executive Officer:** Jack D. Rehm
Group Presidents:
 Joseph J. Ward, Books
 William T. Kerr, Magazines
 Philip A. Jones, Broadcasting
 Allen L. Sabbag, Real Estate
Vice Presidents:
 Leo R. Armatis, Corporate Relations
 Thomas G. Fisher, General Counsel and Secretary
 Larry D. Hartsook, Finance
 Michael A. Sell, Treasurer
 Kathleen J. Zehr, Controller and Assistant Secretary

*All of us at Meredith® Books are dedicated to providing you
with the information and ideas you need to garden
successfully. We guarantee your satisfaction with this book for
as long as you own it. If you have any questions, comments,
or suggestions, please write to us at:*

MEREDITH® BOOKS, Garden Books
Editorial Department, RW 240
1716 Locust St.
Des Moines, IA 50309-3023

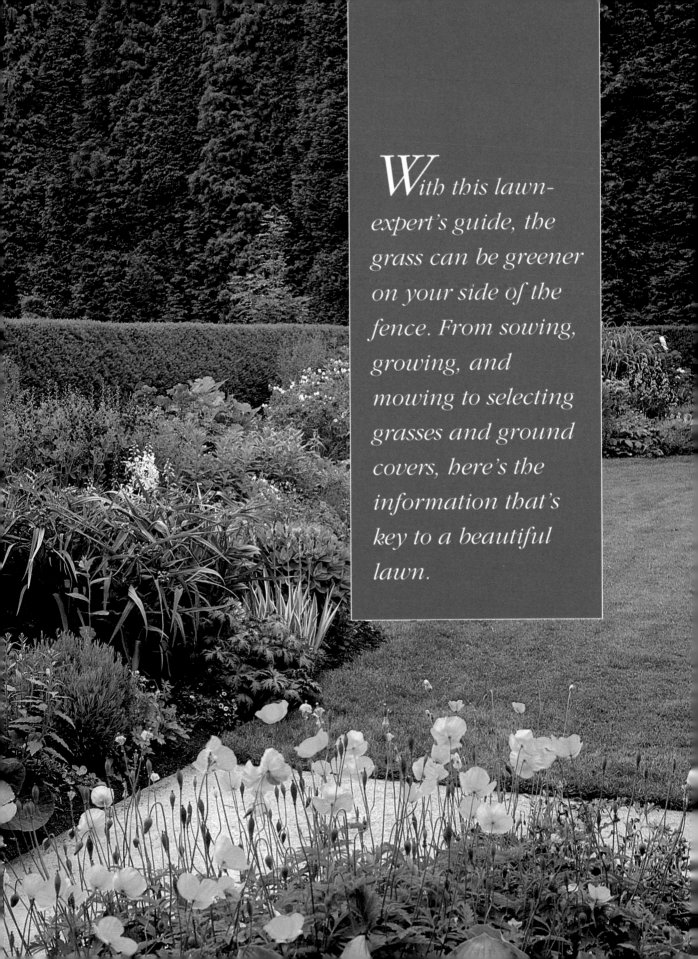

With this lawn-expert's guide, the grass can be greener on your side of the fence. From sowing, growing, and mowing to selecting grasses and ground covers, here's the information that's key to a beautiful lawn.

CONTENTS

STARTING A NEW LAWN 6

LAWN REPAIR AND CARE 16

EASY-CARE LAWN ALTERNATIVES 26

TROUBLESHOOTING TIPS 34

DIRECTORY OF LAWN PLANTS 42

ZONE MAP 62

INDEX 64

Starting a New Lawn

Careful planning is at the root of every lush, easy-care lawn. The right techniques and turf get new lawns off to a healthy start.

Getting Soil in Shape

Just like healthy flower and vegetable gardens, your new lawn needs well-conditioned and well-cultivated soil to produce a rich green carpet of grass that can last for generations.

So, before grasses go in, take time to assess your soil bed. What is the composition of your soil? Will you need to grade the area to level out bumps and slopes for smoother mowing and good drainage? Should you install drainage tile? Does the soil need improvement?

Soil is a mixture of clay, silt, sand, water, organic material, and even living organisms. It can be good or poor, fine or coarse, heavy or light, but whatever kind of soil bed you have in your yard, proper preparation is important to good grass growth.

You can perk up an existing lawn with a little work, but if your lawn has areas of poor soil, dead or neglected turf, terraces that are too steep, or unsatisfactory drainage, then redoing the entire lawn may be in order.

These basic steps can produce a beautiful new lawn.

Checking Soil Needs Loam is ideal soil for growing almost everything. Loam has a texture that holds fertilizer well and drains quickly. It molds into a loose mound when squeezed but crumbles when squeezed harder.

Chances are your soil isn't perfect. It may be high in clay, forming a tight, sticky mass if squeezed when wet. Or, it may be sandy with a grainy feel and, when wet, becomes crumbly.

So, before you cultivate and seed, test for soil type, fertility, and pH levels. Use a do-it-yourself soil test kit or ask your county extension office about testing services in your area.

Most grasses grow best in soil with a neutral or slightly acidic pH that tests between 6 and 7. Add limestone to raise the soil's pH, and powdered sulfur to reduce it.

To remedy clay or sandy soil and boost grass growth, turn soil to a depth of at least 1 foot and add humus with organic matter—peat, weed-free compost, or new topsoil.

Before cultivating, broadcast a balanced fertilizer of nitrogen (preferably slow-release), phosphorus, and potassium, or a specially formulated lawn food.

Making the Grade It's important to make sure the lawn area is relatively level and drains properly. If your yard is small, you can level it with a shovel and a rake. For a larger area, call in a professional with specially designed graders.

The finished lawn should slope away from the house slightly, about ⅛ to ¼ inch per foot, and be contoured so gentle swales conduct excess rainfall to a lower grade. Watch out for depressions that can become waterlogged when it rains. If there's a high water table in your area, it may be wise to install drainage tiles. For steep slopes— more than a 35-degree incline— that can't be graded easily, consider installing a retaining wall or plant the slope in ground cover.

Breaking New Ground Cultivation breaks up soil for seeding and works pre-applied nutrients down to the root zone, where they'll do the most good.

In small yards, a rotary tiller works fine, but in large areas, you'll find plowing or disking with tractor-drawn equipment saves time and effort.

Before cultivating, be sure to remove pieces of plaster, brick, cement, and other debris from the soil bed. Then, cultivate on a day when the soil is suitably moist— not wet enough to cake or clod, but not powder dry either.

Don't overcultivate the soil. The ideal soil bed is cultivated to the point where it has marble-size lumps of soil. Never pulverize soil until it's powdery or dustlike because overcultivated soil "runs" when wet and cakes hard after it dries. You'll find that a pebbled soil surface accepts seed and water best. Seeds germinate quicker when they settle into the cracks and crevices between lumps of soil where moisture and warmth are retained.

Six Easy Steps to a New Lawn

The best time to start a new lawn from seed is early September, when days are cool and moist and weeds are less of a threat. Early spring is second best. Sod, sprigs, and plugs can go in anytime, although spring and fall are preferred. Whatever method you choose, here are the ground rules for growing healthy, attractive turf.

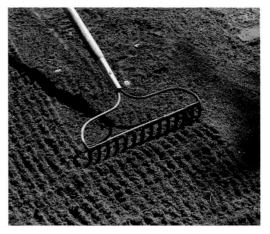

2. After removing stones, twigs, or other debris, level the soil surface with a rake, leaving marble-size lumps. If adding lime to the soil, incorporate before leveling.

1. With a rotary tiller or spade, cultivate the area to 4 inches deep. If soil drains poorly, add 4 to 6 inches of topsoil or sphagnum peat moss and mix well.

3. Apply fertilizer at thr recommended rate, about 2 pounds of nitrogen per 1,000 square feet, with a spreader. Apply half the fertilizer in one direction, the remainder at right angles.

4. Broadcast a high-quality grass seed mixture at the recommended rate, or use another planting method. Roll seed to firm up soil; on slopes, apply burlap or straw to prevent seed from washing away.

5. Water gently to settle the soil after planting. Thereafter, water lightly, but often, to keep the soil moist until seedlings appear. Then water less often, but deeper.

6. When the grass on your newly planted lawn reaches 2 to 2½ inches tall, mow it to a height of 1½ to 2 inches. After that, follow a regular mowing schedule.

Which Grass Should You Choose?

Whether you're seeding, sodding, or using another grass-planting method, establishing a lawn is often a homeowner's largest one-time garden expense, so before you select grasses, consider these factors.

How much traffic will the lawn receive? Some hardy grasses bounce back quickly and are great for children's play areas. Other grasses might look great, but they don't like to be trampled.

What are the growing conditions in all parts of your lawn? Sun, shade, slopes, and areas with weeds all have special needs. Grass seed mixtures can help compensate for variances in your yard. Ask your garden center staff what mixtures are best suited to your yard, and what mixtures have proven successful in your area.

How much maintenance, such as watering, mowing, and fertilizing, do you want to do each year?

What is your budget? If you hire a lawn service, it could cost much more if your grass type needs frequent mowing or feeding.

Match a Mix Generally, the best answer is a grass seed mixture, like most commercial seed. Different types of grasses tolerate different conditions. If disease strikes, the damage probably will be limited to just one of the grasses in the mixture. Some grasses like sun; others, such as fescue varieties, do well in shady spots.

Grasses are usually categorized as cool-season grasses suited to Northern lawns, or warm-season grasses that do well in the South.

Following are some cool-season grasses to consider:

■ Kentucky bluegrass is an unbeatable choice for many lawns because of its dark green color, dense texture, and hardiness. It is found in most cool-season mixes.

■ Fescue is easily grown in most soil conditions and holds up well in dry periods. It is fine-bladed and tolerates shade. Turf-type tall fescues are good for play areas.

■ Ryegrass comes in annual and perennial forms and is favored for rapid growth. Perennial ryegrass grows in most soils and is good in high-traffic areas. Annual ryegrass

can be used as a temporary lawn. It also is used to overseed Bermuda grass in winter in the South.

■ Bent grasses generally don't like the shade and need attention. They grow well in moist, humid climates and provide a putting-green look when clipped under 1 inch.

Some of the warm-season grasses you'll want to consider include:

■ Bermuda grass is good for high-traffic areas and sunny spots. It creeps and must be contained.

■ Dichondra is a popular broadleaf that hugs the ground when grown in the sun. It needs to be watered often.

For easy care, group lawn areas with plants of similar water needs.

■ Bahaia grass is a low-maintenance choice with a long season and will grow in sun or partial shade.

■ Centipede grass withstands drought fairly well and grows in poor soils. It needs little upkeep.

■ St. Augustine grass is an easy-to-maintain type, with coarse texture and a short dormant period.

■ Zoysia grass resists weeds and pests, tolerates most soils, and grows in the shade. It turns brown after a frost.

Lawn Planting Techniques

Choose a turf-planting method based on your grass type, your budget, your climate, and how quickly you want a lawn.

Northern grasses, such as Kentucky bluegrass, fescues, and perennial ryegrasses usually are propagated by seed, although bluegrass sod is a popular way to quick-start a lawn.

In the South, many grasses are planted vegetatively with live stems or sections of sod, using sprigging, plugging, or sodding methods. Common Bermuda grass, centipede grass, carpet grass, and zoysia japonica may be seeded.

Here are guidelines for the best results:

Sprigging Grass sprigs are pieces of stem taken from torn sod. The best sprigs have roots and leaves. Buy sprigs packed in moss from a nursery or garden center, or shred your own sprigs. A square yard of sod may yield more than 1,000 zoysia or Bermuda sprigs. Bury the end of each sprig in soil, covering

Planting grass sprigs

the lowest joint. Plant in furrows or in a checkerboard pattern.

Stolonizing A method of sprigging, stolonizing is broadcasting 5 to 8 bushels of sprigs per 1,000 square feet, then topdressing with soil. Do both sprigging and stolonizing in early spring.

Sodding Popular in the North, sodding is good for slopes or a lawn in a hurry. Bluegrass sod is best. Sod in spring or early fall. Choose thin, weed-free sod rolls, no more than ¾ to 1 inch thick. Lay sod one strip against the next. Lay

Setting grass plugs

Laying sod strips

strips across a hill, not up and down a hill. Topdress with soil and roll.

Seeding with mechanical spreader

Plugging Plugs are small sections of sod, usually circular in shape and often used for warm-climate lawns, such as zoysia or Bermuda grass. Use a plugging tool to make plugs from existing turf. Plant 2- to 4-inch plugs 1 foot apart. A square yard of sod yields around 300 two-inch plugs, enough to plant 40 square yards.

Seeding Where cool-climate grasses flourish, seeding is an option. Buy a high-quality seed mixture. Mulch protects seedlings.

Lawn Repair and Care

*E*ven the best lawns need an occasional pick-me-up. Banish the bare spots, smooth the bumps, and scratch the thatch for health and beauty.

Perk Up an Old Lawn

No matter how bedraggled the weather or general wear and tear leaves your lawn, it has tremendous comeback power. Proper repair and care will quickly improve an existing lawn. The best time is fall in the North and early spring in the South.

Rx for Bare Spots Reseed bare spots in early fall or spring. At other times, use sod or plugs. To seed, prepare the soil by clearing away debris, weeds, and dry grass. Loosen the soil, then add humus and a light application of balanced fertilizer. Rake the soil smooth, spread good seed, and tamp it down. Keep soil moist until seed germinates.

Remove Thatch Check the thatch. Some is good. It recycles plant tissues, adds organic fertilizer, and helps control weeds. But if thatch is more than ¾ inch deep, it can harbor insects and diseases, prevent water and fertilizers from reaching soil, and keep new grass from breaking through. Rent a power rake, and set it deep enough to make small cuts in the soil. Or rake vigorously by hand. You also can use a thatch-removing fertilizer or spray, as directed.

Try Overseeding To give your lawn a new lease on life, overseed after removing thatch. Spread good-quality seed at about half the rate recommended for new lawns—usually 1 or 2 pounds per 1,000 square feet. In southern states, plug warm-season grasses, such as zoysia, into an existing lawn. Before plugging, water the lawn and mow low. Keep soil moist. Mow when grass is 2 inches tall.

Start from Scratch If you decide there's no hope for your existing lawn, then build a new one. First, eliminate existing vegetation by stripping sod or by using a contact herbicide. Check local restrictions on the use of herbicides before applying. Before cultivating, allow the herbicide to work and dissipate. Then, follow the steps in Starting a New Lawn, pages 6–15.

Loosen It Up Weather and high traffic can make compacted soil a problem. Aeration is the answer. Use special aeration equipment—a pitchforklike tool or a spiked roller—to penetrate the soil deeply and remove "cores" of compacted earth from each spike imprint.

Smooth It Out Usually the result of earthworm activity or freezes and thaws, uneven ground hampers mowing and low areas get waterlogged. In low spots, add ¼ inch of weedless topsoil or sand and peat on top of the grass. Rake it smooth. Repeat twice a year until the low spots are filled.

For deep depressions, roll back existing sod in strips about 20 inches wide. Fill holes with clean, rich soil. Smooth and tamp firmly, then replace sod. Topdress with ¼ inch of soil and water deeply.

To lower high spots, use a sharp, flat spade to remove 1-inch-wide, 6-inch-deep wedges of turf the length of the mound. Repeat at 10-inch-wide intervals. Soak area, then use a heavy roller to seal spaces. Repeat in spring and fall until the bump disappears.

Maintaining Your Lawn

The secret to a beautiful lawn is constant, consistent care.

Mowing is a critical part of lawn care and neatness. Match your schedule to the growth rate of your grass. Perhaps every five days in a wet season and every 10 to 14 days during dry times.

Cut your lawn to the ideal height specified for your kind of grass. For bluegrasses, ryegrasses, and fescues, it's about 2 inches during active growth and 3 inches otherwise. Mow bent, Bermuda, and zoysia grasses as low as ¾ to 1¼ inches. Mow tall fescues, St. Augustine grasses, and bahia grass higher, from 3 to 3½ inches.

Mow to Grow Mow often enough to cut only the top third of the blades. This promotes low, thick growth and discourages weeds.

Mow diagonally, alternating directions each time you mow to prevent a striped look and to assure a sharp, even cut. In shady areas, cut the grass higher or mow less often. Sharpen your mower blades at least once a month. If you mow frequently, you can leave the grass clippings on the lawn.

Water Rights Water deeply and thoroughly, 1 inch a week or not at all. Light, frequent sprinklings do more harm than good to an established lawn, encouraging shallow root growth and making grass more vulnerable to damage from drought, weeds, and diseases.

Be sure you are soaking 6 to 12 inches of soil when you water. Sandy soils need less water more often. The more humus you have in your soil, the better it soaks up and retains water. A lawn with fairly heavy soil requires about three hours of watering per week for moisture to penetrate to the proper depth.

Look for signs of lawn stress. A bluish cast, loss of resiliency so footprints show, and slow growth indicate thirst. During long periods of little or no rainfall, community water shortages may force you to stop outdoor watering. Allowing grass to go dormant may be your only defense against drought. Even

if grass goes dormant for a summer, it usually greens up again as soon as the rains return.

Feed and Weed Proper applications of fertilizer make grass plants strong and healthy so they can withstand drought and traffic and crowd out weeds. In spring, use a fertilizer with a 2-1-1 ratio of nitrogen to phosphorus and potash. In fall, use a fertilizer with a 1-2-2 ratio for healthy root growth in winter. Apply about 4 pounds per

A beautiful lawn takes time, water, and work.

1,000 square feet. Granular, slow-release fertilizers work well, or use a water-soluble type applied with a hose sprayer.

For extensive weeding, use weed killers carefully as directed. Never spray on a windy day. Label the sprayer "For Herbicides Only." When weeds are few, remove them by hand, using a long-handled asparagus cutter.

Turf-Care Shortcuts

Lighten lawn maintenance, make mowing easier, and create a more attractive yard by trying a few of these time-tested tips:

Tree Tricks Plant trees in groups, in swaths of mulch or ground cover, or in gardens. A lawn dotted with trees is a challenge to mow.

Lop Limbs Prune lower limbs from trees. It's easier to walk under them when you mow, and pruning opens your lawn to more sunlight.

Power Strips Install mowing strips: low-to-the-ground bands of concrete, brick, or other material on which the mower wheel can travel. Locate sprinkler heads in the center of the bands to keep them out of the mower's path.

Sharper Edge Good edging creates a finished look for the lawn and protects trees from nicks. Neatly define flower beds, borders, and mulched trees and shrubs with edgings of wood, vinyl, brick, or other materials.

Easy-Care Redo Design your lawn so that you can easily get the mower from one area to another. When reducing the lawn size with other plantings, don't leave islands of grass.

Keep It Clean Don't let leaves, lawn furniture, toys, or other objects remain on the lawn any longer than necessary. The grass beneath them will quickly lose color and may die.

Timely Tasks Do lawn chores promptly. Mow before the lawn needs raking, fertilize before it needs reseeding, and treat pests and diseases before extensive damage occurs.

Turf-Care Tools Yard tool choices should depend on the size and makeup of your yard, as well as your temperament and the time you have for yard work.

Today there's a wide range of mowers, edgers, weed cutters, leaf blowers, rakes, spades, spreaders, and hand tools on the market.

Match the tools you buy to your lawn and garden needs. For example, if the lawn is large and you have little time, a riding mower will speed work.

Examine tools before you buy. If a handle is too long, short, or heavy for you, try another. Check connections. The strongest spades, forks, and shovels include a metal shank part way up the handle.

Choose hoses for weight, length, durability, and ease of repair. Consider soaker hoses, mist nozzles, and sprinklers according to your needs. Wind up hoses between use. Excessive sun shortens their life. Drain hoses well before winter.

Clean tools after each use. Wipe wooden handles with linseed oil. Paint them a bright color if you tend to lose tools. Sharpen tools; check and tighten bolts for efficiency and safety.

Remove grass clippings, dirt, and grease from your mower and keep the blades sharp. Before storing for the winter, run the mower until the

A tool shed close to the garden saves energy and time.

gasoline is used. Drain the crankcase. Clean the oil filter. Add clean oil.

Sharpen blades of shears, mowers, spades, and hoes before winter storage. Apply oil, floor wax, or petroleum jelly.

Store all sprays, dusts, and poisons out of the reach of children and pets.

Landscape Calendar

Outdoor tasks to keep your landscape in top shape may differ in different regions of the country, but scheduling care is important. Here's a season-spanning checklist for cold-winter climates:

January/February: Sweep snow off evergreens before branches break. Use de-icing salt sparingly.

March: Prune early-flowering shrubs after they bloom. Remove old leaves from beds in stages on dark days. Plant grass for new or repaired lawns. Check outdoor structures.

April: Clean up yard. Spread compost around trees and shrubs. Begin mowing when grass reaches 2½ inches. Spread preemergent herbicide to control crabgrass.

May: Give new trees and shrubs a deep watering.

June: Water lawn as needed. Spread and deepen mulch. Sweep decks and patios often. Prune pine candles (new growth) to half their length; prune other evergreens to desired size. Trim deciduous hedges before growth hardens.

July/August: Set mower blade higher in dry weather.

September: This is the best time for seeding or repairing lawns. Combine post- and preemergent herbicide. Plant trees and shrubs in mild climates. Check and repair outdoor structures before winter.

October: Rake leaves; compost or use as mulch. Bag some leaves for insulation around foundations.

November/December: Clean, oil tools. Spray evergreens, Christmas trees, and treasured plants with antitranspirant spray to reduce the drying effects of cold wind. Save wood ashes from fireplace to add to soil next spring.

For warm-winter climates, here's a list of outdoor tasks:

January/February: Spray full-strength dormant oil on fruit and deciduous trees; use half-strength spray on broad-leaved evergreens. Prepare lawn furniture and tools for spring.

March: Feed lawn; mow grass when it's above 2½ inches high. Check structures for damage.

April: Feed lawn; aerate it anytime. Spread mulch. Prune spring-flowering shrubs after bloom. Shorten pine candles (new growth); prune evergreens before growth starts.

May: Sow seed, lay sod, or plant plugs of warm-season grasses now through summer. Keep watered until settled.

June: Prune and thin spring-blooming shrubs. Watch for insects; wash or pick them off before they can multiply. Use fungicide where diseases usually are a problem. Mow lawn as needed; dethatch now for fast recovery; treat chinch bugs.

July: Water and work outdoors in early morning or evening. Sweep

Schedule and pace outdoor chores to fit your lifestyle.

deck and patio often. Check evergreens for insect pests.

August: Give last trim to deciduous and evergreen hedges.

September: Make major lawn repairs; feed and lime old lawns.

October: Gather and compost or bag leaves. Continue to mow so grass won't be too long heading into winter.

November/December: Use herbicide for winter weeds when lawn is dormant. Update your landscape plan; assess and make any needed changes. Clean and oil your lawn-care tools.

Easy-Care Lawn Alternatives

*F*or hard-to-mow, hard-to-grow spots, try attractive ground covers, practical mulches, and native plants for a great change.

Versatile Ground Covers

Colorful and easy to maintain, ground covers can play a vital role in your landscape. They're hard workers, too, spreading fast to fill in trouble spots.

Ground covers often are used for an attractive carpet around trees and shrubs where grasses fare poorly. But they also reduce weeds, conserve soil moisture, control slope erosion, and accent elements, such as stepping-stones, garden walls, and shady, rocky areas.

In selecting ground covers, consider light, climate, moisture, soil, and the ground cover's role. Many, such as goutweed, crown vetch, and sedum, tolerate poor soil and dryness. Fill in rocky walls with thrift, candytuft, or pearlwort, for example.

Low-growing plants, such as pearlwort, creeping thyme, sedum, and baby's-tears, thrive between stepping-stones. On hills, choose ground cover with a heavy root system, such as ivy, hosta, or ice plant. Alpine strawberries, pachysandra, and periwinkle or vinca minor help control erosion.

A tough spot for grass-growing and mowing, this slope is now an eye-catcher with colorful blooms that change with the seasons.

For bright foliage, try silver snow-in-summer, blue fescue, or purple winter creeper. Colorful bloomers include gold alyssum, white candytuft, and purple liriope. Near windows and decks, choose a fragrant cover, such as lily-of-the-valley. Or, plant a carpet of edible alpine strawberries.

Plant ground covers in spring or fall. Although many resist drought, they do best when adequately watered. Use a complete fertilizer in early spring; mulch semihardy types in fall in cold-winter areas.

Deep, under-the-trees shade doesn't stop the hardy hostas from thriving. With a variety of foliage shapes, sizes, and textures to choose from, this perennial ground cover is a natural around trees and walkways, eliminating the need to mow.

In May, drifts of white candytuft and gold alyssum edge the shady, sloping path to this home.

No-Mow Options

More than 150 kinds of grasses grow in the United States. Among them are ornamental varieties that provide showy displays and don't need mowing.

Most fancy grasses have long, slender leaves and, if any, tiny flowers. To landscapes, the grasses add delicacy, soft colors, or plumelike flower clusters.

Grow annual grasses from seeds sown in spring in open, sunny areas. Start perennial grasses from transplants or root divisions. Don't overcrowd plants. Start a sampling of decorative grasses in a back corner of your yard to find your favorites.

In small spaces, try modest terrace displays of small grasses, such as fescue, Japanese sedge, and quaking grasses. Blue fescue is a beauty in formal gardens, arranged in bouquet-size mounds in geometric patterns. Ribbon grass with green-and-white striped blades and green-and-yellow zebra grass grow quickly. Pampas grass isn't winter-hardy; northern gardeners should lift and store the roots.

Making the Most of Mulches

Mulching is one of the best things you can do for your garden, trees, and shrubs. It helps soil retain moisture, keeps weeds down, prevents mower nicks to trees, and tidies up areas that are hard to mow, grow, and weed.

It's a wonderful way to recycle, too. Organic mulches slowly rot to improve soil. Use the free mulches from your yard and garden, or buy mulches from a garden center.

Here are some common mulches, recommended application, and comments on their uses:

■ Bark: Shredded, lay 2 inches deep; attractive and long lasting but can be expensive.

■ Corncobs: Ground, lay 3 inches deep; a good choice, slightly acidic.

■ Cottonseed hulls: 3-inch depth; nice appearance but tends to scatter. Keep moist.

■ Grass clippings: 2-inch depth; free, effective, an earthworm favorite. Replenish often. Compost grass sprayed with weed killer before using as mulch.

■ Leaves: 2-inch depth; shred before using. Most break down rapidly and attract earthworms.

■ Pine needles: 3-inch depth; easy to use, slightly acidic, and prone to burning. Hold up well and drain freely. Pine boughs make superb winter mulch.

Ornamental grasses make dramatic edgings or accents.

■ Plastic: Black or clear, 6 mils. Water ground before laying, cut holes for plants. Excellent for plants that like warm soil.

■ Straw: 4-inch depth; superb summer or winter. Attracts worms.

■ Stone or rock: 2-inch depth; nice texture and shape. Loose rock can be a problem along paths and in borders.

Easy-Living Landscapes

Tired of spending Saturday mornings mowing your lawn? Then go native by picking plants indigenous to your region or by turning your yard into a no-mow meadow.

Medieval cottages had yards that were a profusion of blooms, replicated in today's popular wildflower gardens. In areas prone to drought, native plants can survive where others fail because they've adapted to the climate. In desert regions with lots of heat and little water, careful plant selection of jade, aloe, ice plant, and cactus can turn a barren yard into an exotic oasis. In deep-shade areas,

try rock gardens dotted with lush ground cover.

Whatever your yard's special needs, planting an easy-living lawn is not only environment-friendly but also may add personality to your landscape. The adobe-and-wood architecture of the southwestern house opposite serves as the backdrop for the unrefined habits of native sage mixed with daylily. Fairy roses, in the foreground, lend a civilized air.

Flowering Lawns If you love flowers and don't like to mow the lawn, roll back the sod and plant a crazy-quilt mixture of quick-growing annuals and perennials. Once established, these hardy flowers will choke out most weeds. The welcoming yard above right includes evening primrose, nasturtium, delphinium, cranesbill geranium, and shasta daisy.

When the yard at right was leveled for easier mowing, it left an abrupt grade change. The answer was a well-designed rock garden that holds the slope beautifully.

Troubleshooting Tips

*E*ven well-tended lawns may fall victim to weeds and to pest and insect damage. Here are common problems and yard-tested solutions.

Weed Invaders

CHICKWEED, MOUSE-EAR
Cerastium vulgatum

Comments: Creeping perennial likes moist, cool conditions. Forms dense mat, with tiny white flowers from April into October. Grows almost everywhere.

Controls: Hard to pull; apply a post-emergent herbicide.

CRABGRASS, COMMON
Digitaria sanguinalis

Comments: Annual bunch grass common except in Southwest and southern Florida. Blooms July to October; likes moisture and sun.

Controls: Mow lawn high in spring to shade seedlings; apply a pre-emergent control in early spring.

DANDELION
Taraxacum officinale

Comments: The most common perennial broadleaf; common except in Deep South. Produces coarse-toothed leaves, yellow blooms, then round white seed heads. In cold areas, flowers from March until freeze; in warm areas, flowers year-round.

Controls: Dig taproot. Use a post-emergent herbicide in fall. Spot chemical applicators available.

DOCK, CURLY
Rumex crispus

Comments: Perennial with 1½- to 2-foot taproot, one or more tall stems. Common across country. Spikes of whitish flowers from June into September.

Controls: Dig entire taproot. Or, apply post-emergent herbicide; spray into each plant crown.

LAMB'S-QUARTERS
Chenopodium album

Comments: Common annual on newly seeded lawns or thin turf. Leaves white on underside. Plume-like, whitish flower heads and seeds appear June to October.

Controls: Mow lawn closely. Soak soil for easy pulling, or use post-emergent herbicide.

PLANTAIN, BROAD-LEAF
Plantago major

Comments: Common perennial (sometimes annual) with broad leaves, 3 to 6 inches long, bunched low to the ground. Tall stalks bear pencil-shape flowers from June to October. Self-seeds.

Controls: Dig when soil is moist. In large areas, use post-emergent herbicide in early spring or fall.

QUACK GRASS

Agropyron repens

Comments: Also called couch grass, this vigorous-spreading perennial bunchgrass is common except in parts of Southwest and Deep South. Forms a dense root structure by rooting at every joint on underground stems.

Controls: Cannot be eradicated without killing lawn grasses, too. A black plastic cover over a patch will starve growth. Or apply a post-emergent control; wait three weeks before reseeding lawn.

SHEPHERD'S PURSE

Capsella bursa-pastoris

Comments: Persistent annual low leaves, white flowers on tall stems. Flat, heart-shape seedpods.

Controls: Fairly easy to pull if soil is moist. In large areas, use post-emergent herbicide.

THISTLE, CANADA

Cirsium arvense

Comments: Thrives in clay soils in the North. Long, prickly leaves, with lavender flowers July through

Spot-treat weeds on a calm day if you're using herbicide sprays.

October. Thistle spreads by seeds and roots.

Controls: Use knife to cut below ground and remove crown from roots. For larger infestation, apply a post-emergent herbicide.

YARROW, COMMON

Achillea millefolium

Comments: Also called milfoil, creeping perennial with very finely divided leaves and white, cushiony blooms. Common in poor soil in most regions, except Southwest. Spreads by seeds and underground stems.

Controls: Dig out as soon as it appears. For larger area, control with a couple of applications of post-emergent herbicide.

Lawn Insects

ARMYWORMS, CUTWORMS

Trouble Signs: These pests are found in dense groups feeding on grass at soil level, leaving dead spots. Armyworms grow to 1½ inches long with green, tan, or black stripes. Cutworms grow 2 inches long, are gray or brown, and smooth. Damage occurs spring through late summer.

Controls: Keep lawn healthy by watering and feeding on schedule. At first sign, spray lawn with 1 cup liquid dish soap per 10 gallons of water. If damage persists, use *bacillus thuringiensis.*

BILLBUGS

Trouble Signs: One of the top four lawn pests, they chew holes in grass stems to deposit eggs. Larvae puncture stem and crown as they feed. These black or red-brown beetles grow ¼ to ¾ inch long. They kill grass in irregular patches; grass blades break off at soil line. Worst mid-June through July.

Controls: In lawns with a history of billbug damage, treat with diazinon or carbaryl to control adults in early spring. Or, treat to control larvae in early summer.

CHINCH BUGS

Trouble Signs: Another least-wanted pest, feeds at all stages of development, leaving large, yellowish-to-brown patches in grass. Adults have black bodies, white wings, reddish legs, and grow to ⅓ inch long. They attack cool-season grasses in early summer and again in September. Wilts or kills St. Augustine grass.

Controls: Keep lawns well fed; control thatch. Treat in June and August with bendiocarb, diazinon, ethoprop, or chlorpyrifos.

GRUBS, WHITE

Trouble Signs: Grubs eat grass roots, leaving brown, dead patches easily lifted out of the lawn and repaired. Grubs are the larvae of beetles, including Japanese and June. Larvae are thick, whitish, C-shape underground worms that vary from ¾ to 1½ inches long.

Controls: Cut sections of sod; pick off grubs from the underside of sod and destroy them. Or control with diazinon or isofenphos, as directed. Treat grubs of Japanese beetle with milky spore disease.

LEAFHOPPERS

Trouble Signs: These yellow, brown, or green slender, wedge-shape insects are less than ½ inch long. They suck juices from leaves, causing grass to turn white, then yellow, then brown. They flit away as you walk past. Common, but especially active on East and West coasts. Seldom serious pests.

Controls: Treat with soapy water and tobacco juice (soak chewing tobacco in an old stocking in a pint of hot water overnight). Use diazinon if needed.

MITES

Trouble Signs: Clover mites are tiny, red specks found in lawns across the country. Bermuda grass mites are pale green and microscopic and attack Gulf Coast and western lawns. All spiderlike mites suck leaf juices. Grass wilts, yellows, and dies.

Controls: Avoid heavy feeding; succulent grass growth attracts mites. Control with diazinon.

MOLE CRICKETS

Trouble Signs: Brownish insects eat roots, stems, other bugs, and earthworms and leave irregular, brown patches. About 1½ inches long; prefer bahia grass and warm, moist conditions.

Controls: Spread diatomaceous earth mixed with cheap laundry soap over turf. Or treat with diazinon.

SOD WEBWORM

Trouble Signs: One of the most common and damaging lawn insects. Tan moths, about ¾ inch long, fly just above grass at dusk, laying eggs. Gray, tan, or green larvae, up to 1 inch long, feed on shots and crowns of blue-bent and zoysia grasses and fescues, causing irregular, close-clipped brown patches. As many as three generations in a season: May, July, and September.

Controls: Mow and water well a day before treating with *bacillus thuringiensis*, bendiocarb, chlorpyrifos, diazinon, or ethoprop. Spray late in the day. Don't mow or water for 48 hours.

NOTE: Your county extension office has information about recommended insecticides and applications. Use a chemical only as a last resort.

Lawn Diseases

BROWN PATCH

Attacks: All grasses in the Midwest; rye-, bent, blue-, and St. Augustine grasses in southern coastal areas.

Signs and Controls: Circular brown spots from 1 inch to several feet. Leaves first look brown and water soaked, then dry. Ryegrass appears slimy. Fungi live in plant debris. Symptoms appear suddenly when humidity and night temperatures are high. Disease thrives on excessive thatch and nitrogen. Use slow release or reduced nitrogen fertilizer in spring. Water mornings only. Apply lime if needed. Remove and discard clippings. Reduce shade; improve aeration and drainage.

COTTONY BLIGHT, PYTHIUM BLIGHT

Attacks: Lawn grasses in damp soil in hot, humid areas.

Signs and Controls: Check for masses of cottony fungi in lawn. Fungi best seen in dampness of early morning. Reduce nitrogen, improve drainage, and increase air circulation by pruning or thinning surrounding shrubs. Reseed.

DOLLAR SPOT

Attacks: Bent grasses are most susceptible. Also infects Kentucky bluegrass, fescues, and Bermuda, zoysia, and St. Augustine grasses.

Signs and Controls: Primary disease with spots the size of silver dollars, often running together to form irregular areas. Kills grass. Feed grass spring and fall; apply frequent, light nitrogen. Destroy clippings. Avoid Nugget and Sydsport bluegrass cultivars. Fungicide may help.

FAIRY RINGS

Attacks: These fungi don't attack grass directly but interfere with the roots' intake of water, oxygen, and nutrients.

Signs and Controls: A circular ring from a few inches to 50 feet in diameter, often with darker green grass inside and mushrooms around edges. To control, soak and feed area with garden root feeder. Remove thatch, aerate, or use a wetting agent to help water penetrate. Replacing infested sod or fumigating are the only ways to eliminate and are expensive.

FUSARIUM BLIGHT

Attacks: Common and often serious in bluegrass; less so in red fescue and bent grasses.

Signs and Controls: Most likely in central states and Northeast, especially in hot, dry, windy weather. Small tan spots appear in early summer and may merge. Crown of dead plants can appear brown or black. Use resistant seed or sod. Water thoroughly. Apply wetting agent to ensure deep soaking of root zone. Remove thatch and avoid excess nitrogen.

LEAF SPOTS

Attacks: Bermuda, St. Augustine, and bent grasses and fescues.

Signs and Controls: Fungus spreads fast in warm, humid, rainy weather. Little brown spots on grass blades, then spread into long areas with gray centers, purple, water-logged edges. Grass looks scorched. Avoid quick-release nitrogen; use slow-release ureaform.

MELTING OUT

Attacks: Especially bluegrass.

Signs and Controls: Small, round, gray, brown, or purplish black spots on leaf blades spread to kill leaves and roots. Most common during high temperatures and humidity, and on closely cropped lawns. Don't mow too low. Avoid excess spring nitrogen. Reduce shade; improve aeration and drainage. Use fungicides.

RUST

Attacks: Bluegrasses, ryegrasses, and Bermuda, zoysia, and St. Augustine grasses.

Signs and Controls: Rust-colored blisters on leaves cause plants to wither and die. When blisters burst, spores spread. Mow lawn weekly and catch and destroy clippings. Maintain fertility. Promote good growth by regular feeding and watering.

SNOW MOLD

Attacks: Cool-season grasses. Affects low areas. Snow not required for pink snow mold.

Signs and Controls: Pink fungal strands seen early morning around patches 6 inches to several feet in diameter. Cut lawn shorter in fall, remove clippings. Don't fertilize in late fall—after August 15 to September 15.

Directory of Lawn Plants

Create a custom landscape plan by matching lawn grasses and ground covers to the needs of your home, your climate, and your lifestyle.

Cool-Season Grasses

BENT GRASSES
Agrostis sp.

Colonial
A. tenuis

Velvet
A. canina

Creeping
A. stolonifera

Description: Most species produce turf that is shiny green, thick, and fine-textured.

Light: Sun

Mowing Height: ¾ inch

Comments: Fine bents are mainly used by golf greenskeepers and are not recommended for home lawns unless you're willing to spend the effort required for regular watering, feeding, spraying, and mowing with a reel mower. Adapted for use in cool, humid climates. Tolerates light shade.

Redtop
A. gigantea

Description: A coarse stemmy form of bent grass. Differs from all other bent grasses in its beautiful, fine-textured effect.

Light: Sun

Mowing Height: 1½–2 inches

Comments: Tolerates some shade, only in hot summer areas. Adapted to moist conditions and range of soils. Persists on dry, coarse soils. Doesn't tolerate much traffic. Under heat stress, it turns brown. Main advantage as temporary cover. Not used in top-quality lawn seed mixtures.

BLUEGRASSES
Poa sp.

Common Kentucky
P. pratensis

Description: Hardy, sod-forming perennial grass; dark green blades with V-shape leaf tips. Blades upright; fine-textured soft growth. Extensive root system penetrates soil 3 to 4 feet.

Light: Sun

Mowing Height: 1½–2½ inches

Comments: Main grass for lawns in North but also grows in cool, mountain altitudes in South. Has upright blade so turf is not dense;

blends well with other bluegrasses. Looks best during spring and fall. Grass goes dormant during hot, dry summers; greens up in cool, moist weather. It is disease-prone in certain conditions. Many new cultivars being derived from common Kentucky bluegrass.

Delta

Description: More erect, stiffer blades, but less dense than Kentucky bluegrass.

Light: Sun

Mowing Height: 1½–3 inches

Comments: Tolerates drought more than some others; resists most diseases fairly well. Establishes and greens up well in spring.

Fylking

Description: Medium-fine texture, dark green color, low growth habit.

Light: Sun

Mowing Height: 1½–2 inches

Comments: Good resistance to most diseases. Proves drought resistant and handles low temperatures. Grows in sandy soils.

Merion Kentucky

Description: Denser than Kentucky bluegrass; blue-green color.

Light: Sun

Mowing Height: ¾-1 inch

Comments: Considered an improvement over Kentucky bluegrass but somewhat slow to germinate. Susceptible to rust disease; resists leaf spot. Demands extra feeding. Tolerates some shade.

Newport

Description: Dark green with medium coarse texture similar to Merion. Growth habit similar to Kentucky.

Light: Sun

Mowing Height: 1½–3 inches

Comments: Requires less fertilizer than Merion. Not as tolerant of low temperatures, drought. Susceptible to several diseases.

Park

Description: Produces vigorous seedlings. Similar to common bluegrass in growth habit. Medium dark green color. Forms dense sod.

Light: Sun

Mowing Height: 1½–3 inches

Comments: Has good drought tolerance and good spring, green-up rate. Fairly good resistance to most diseases.

Rough-stalk meadow-grass

P. trivialis

Description: Shiny, apple-green colored turf with high shoot density. Smaller stemmed than common Kentucky.

Light: Shade

Mowing Height: 1½ inches

Comments: Grow in shade only; avoid sandy soil. Does not tolerate heat and drought. Adapted to cool, moist areas. Tolerates low temperatures.

Windsor

Description: Bright, blue-green leaf blades. Plants tend to creep. Low-lying; dense turf.

Light: Sun

Mowing Height: ¾ –1½ inches

Comments: Although it can be mowed shorter than Kentucky because of its low habit, 1½-inch mowing height works best. Start lawns by seed. Vigorous; drought and disease resistant. A versatile, attractive bluegrass.

FESCUES
Festuca sp.

Coarse, tall fescues

F. elatior

Description: Alta or Kentucky-31 and Goar are all medium coarse, tall, tough fescues. Leaves are large, medium green in color, and grow in clumps.

Light: Light shade

Mowing Height: 2–2½ inches

Comments: Useful mostly for play areas that get rough treatment. Sow as a pure stand and at hearty rate for finer texture. Disease and drought resistant.

Fine, Red creeping

F. rubra

Description: Highlight, Jamestown, Koket, and Ruby are commonly used cultivars. They form a very fine-textured grass, which is medium to dark green in color. More and improved cultivars are being released. Chewings fescue is similar to red fescues, except it does not creep and it's tufty.

Light: Shade

Mowing Height: 2–2½ inches

Comments: Adapts well to shade. Needs little nitrogen. Is drought resistant and grows in dry, sandy soils. Used in some commercial lawn seed mixtures. Although it germinates faster than bluegrass, it is compatible with it in mixtures. It is more susceptible to disease than coarse fescues.

RYEGRASSES
Lolium sp.

Annual, Italian
L. multiflorum

Description: Large-seeded and germinates rapidly to show green growth in a few days. Blades are coarser than bluegrass.

Light: Sun

Mowing Height: 1½ inches

Comments: Useful for quick green cover for a season. It dies out, mostly, in one year. It is often used for overseeding Bermuda grass lawns in the South for green cover over winter. Will not live over summer in South or winter in North.

Perennial
L. perenne

Description: It has coarse, sparsely set blades that have a waxy sheen. It is not quite as coarse as annual rye.

Light: Sun or light shade

Mowing Height: 1½ inches

Comments: Cultivars such as Citation, Compas, Derby, Game, Manhattan, NK-100, NK-200, Omega, Pennfine, or Yorktown should be used. Many of the cultivars have a fine-textured appearance almost equal to that of bluegrass. It is often sown in mixture with bluegrass. It becomes established faster than bluegrass or fescue. It doesn't mow as neatly as bluegrass.

Southern Warm-Season Grasses

BAHAIA GRASS
Paspalum notatum

Description: Very coarse textured, fairly open, erect, and tough. One of widest-leaved species. Spreads slowly by stolons and roots.

Light: Sun

Mowing Height: 2–3 inches

Comments: Tolerates partial shade. Turns brown at 30 degrees Fahrenheit. Limited to warm areas where low maintenance desired. Popular varieties in southern coastal region are Argentine and Pensacola. Start by seed or sod. Feed three times a year. Mow often enough to remove wiry seed stalks.

Fancy maiden grass bears plumes, and there's no mowing required.

BERMUDA GRASS
Cynodon dactylon

Description: Hybrid forms are most beautiful and provide a dense, fine-textured carpet. U-3 is medium-fine textured, dark green turf with gray cast. Tifdwarf has miniature leaves. Tifgreen is dark green and very fine-textured. Tiflawn is dark green and medium fine. Tifway is medium fine with very dark green leaves. Sunturf is a high-quality, very fine, dark green turf. Ormond is fine-textured with a blue-green color. Santa Ana is medium textured with blue-green leaves.

Light: Sun

Mowing Height: ¾–1 inch

Comments: Bermuda grasses are vigorous and spread by creeping.

Unless contained, they become a weed, invading flower beds. Propagate by sprigs, plugs, or sod. Tiflawn cultivar is tough, wear-resistant in heavy traffic. Tifgreen tolerates partial shade. U-3 tolerates cooler regions of upper South. Tifdwarf requires less frequent mowing. Tifway keeps color late into the fall throughout South. Sunturf, Ormond, and Santa Ana are especially adapted to California, being smog and salt resistant. Feed Bermuda lawns every two months in Deep South, but about four times a year in other regions. Mow common Bermuda lawns higher than hybrids, at least 1 inch.

CARPET GRASS
Axonopus affinis

Description: Growth habit similar to centipede grass. Coarse texture; fairly dense, light green color.

Light: Sun

Mowing Height: 1–2 inches

Comments: Although it doesn't make a good turf, it takes hard wear and needs little attention. Adapted to lower South into upper South. Commonly started by seed but can use sprigs spaced 6 to 12 inches apart. Feed at least once a year. Mow often enough to prevent unsightly seed stalks.

CENTIPEDE GRASS
Eremochloa ophiuroides

Description: Slow-growing, medium-textured grass that spreads by creeping stems and rooting as they go. Seldom grows to 4 inches tall. Medium green color.

Light: Sun

Mowing Height: 1½ inches

Comments: Commonly started by sprigs or plugs spaced 6 to 12 inches apart. Similar to St. Augustine grass, but will grow in cooler parts of warm, humid regions. Not as tolerant of drought as other southern grasses; discolors more readily at low temperatures. Needs little fertilizer and seldom needs mowing. Avoid seashore environment and heavy traffic. Water regularly.

ST. AUGUSTINE GRASS
Stenotaphrum secundatum

Description: Produces broad, flat stems and coarse, attractive blue-green leaves. Establishes and spreads fairly fast in warm, humid regions of lower South. Highly rated variety is Bitter-Blue.

Light: Sun or light shade

Mowing Height: 1½–2 inches

Comments: Propagates readily by sprigs, plugs, or sod. Space sprigs 6 to 12 inches apart. Stays green all year in warmer sections of warm, humid climates. Loses color during winter in other areas but can be sprayed with green dye. Maintains good color with occasional feeding. Will grow in sun but is used widely because it tolerates shade well, even dense shade. Main problem is insects and fungal diseases. Helps to dethatch turf once a year.

ZOYSIA GRASSES
Zoysia sp.

Manila *Z. matrella*

Mascarene *Z. tenuifolia*

Korean or Japanese *Z. japonica*

Description: Manila grass is similar to the finer Japanese. Mascarene has bright green leaves. Japanese or Korean grass has coarse, upright, gray-green leaves. Emerald and hardy Meyer cultivars have fine, dark green blades not unlike Kentucky bluegrass. Produce thickest of turfs.

Light: Sun

Mowing Height: ¾–1½ inches

Comments: Adapted to warm section of approximate southern half of the United States. Most are susceptible to drought. Used in mild East and West coastal regions for seaside lawns because tolerant of salt air. Meyer zoysia grows into zone 5; turns brown after first frost in northern parts of its limit, greens up in May. Emerald is more cold resistant than other zoysias and stays green in frost-free areas of South. Crabgrass, weeds, and bluegrass are crowded out. Susceptible to brown patch, dollar spot, and various insects. Tolerates some shade. Space sprigs or plugs 6 inches apart in spring. Feed spring and fall. Mow Japanese zoysia 1½ inches, mascarene and Manila ¾ to 1 inch.

Western Great Plains Dryland Grasses

BLUE GRAMA GRASS
Bouteloua gracilis

Description: Gray-green, slightly hairy leaves grow in low tufts, merging as they enlarge.

Light: Sun

Mowing Height: 2–3 inches

Comments: Propagation mainly by seed. More desirable where quality of turf is not important. A low-maintenance grass. Heat and drought resistant.

BUFFALO GRASS
Buchloe dactyloides

Description: Fine-textured, soft, low-growing, gray-green grass of fairly good density. Distinctive curling leaf blades. Turns straw color in high temperatures.

Light: Full sun

Mowing Height: ½–1½ inches

Comments: Good where good-quality lawns are not possible because of drought and alkaline soil in Great Plains. Does not survive where rainfall is more than 25 inches a year. Minimum rainfall is 12 inches. Low maintenance. Grown from seeds, sprigs, or plugs.

Ground Covers

BABY'S-TEARS, ANGEL'S-TEARS
Soleirolia soleiroli

Zone: 10

Description: Creeping runners give dense cover of shiny ⅛-inch, rounded green leaves.

Light: Shade

Comments: Best in rich, moist soil, light to deep shade, and in small areas, such as under trees or shrubs. Set 6 to 12 inches apart. Start any time of year, add compost to soil, and water regularly until well-established.

BEARBERRY, KINNIKINICK
Arctostaphylos uva-ursi

Zone: 2 10

Description: Wide-spreading evergreen shrub 6 to 12 inches tall. Shiny, dark green leaves about 1 inch long. Bright red berries attract birds.

Light: Sun or light shade

Comments: Sandy, acid soil; seaside or mountains. Space plants 1 to 2 feet apart in early spring or late fall.

BIRD'S-FOOT TREFOIL
Lotus corniculatus

Zone: 3–10

Description: Three ½-inch leaflets per leaf stem. Grows 1 to 2 feet tall. Is evergreen in warmer areas. Yellow pea blooms are followed by clawlike pods.

Light: Sun or light shade

Comments: Tolerates poor soil, but needs good drainage. Best used to cover large areas. Sow seed at rate of 2 pounds per 1,000 square feet. Or set plants 6 inches apart in spring or summer. Mow like a lawn for even, compact growth.

BISHOP'S WEED, GOUTWEED

Aegopodium podagraria variegatum'

Zone: 3–10

Description: Grows 8 to 10 inches high. Mass of green and white leaves with cluster of white flowers in midsummer. Spreads rapidly by underground stolons. Freeze kills tops in fall with new growth each spring.

Light: Shade or partial sun

Comments: Will grow in almost any soil. Avoid hot sun, winds. Best in contained situation where rampant growth won't crowd other areas. Will grow under most trees and shrubs. Plant in spring or early fall; space plants 6 to 10 inches apart. Grown mainly for attractive foliage. Cut off flower stalks to maintain neat appearance. Easy to lift, separate, and replant from established plantings.

BLUE FESCUE

Festuca ovina 'glauca'

Zone: 3–9

Description: Grows 4 to 10 inches high in compact mounds of whitish-blue blades. Attractive year-round.

Light: Shade or part sun

Comments: Thrives in most soils but best in poor, fairly dry soil. Tolerates seashore planting and windy exposures. Space plants 6 inches apart for tight appearance and 10 to 12 inches apart for loose appearance.

CARPET BUGLE, BUGLEWEED

Ajuga reptans

Zone: 3–10

Description: Produces deep green, 2- to 4-inch shiny leaves, forming rosettes flat on ground or up to 5 to 6 inches high. Blue flower spikes in spring rise 4 to 6 inches above foliage. Turns bronzy red in fall. Several cultivars with multicolored leaves available.

Light: Sun or light shade

Carpet bugle, or bugleweed

Comments: Considered one of the best low-growing ground covers. Although it prefers sunlight or partial sunlight, it can be useful in deep shade. Prefers moist, enriched soil. Multicolored cultivars useful in self-contained edging around patios or front entrances. Space plants 6 to 12 inches apart. Keep watered in hot, dry weather. Feed in early spring to keep cover dense. Make sure plants don't smother over winter from wet leaves; cover lightly with brush or evergreen prunings.

CHAMOMILE, ENGLISH, OR ROMAN CHAMOMILE
Chamaemelum nobile

Zone: 3–10

Description: Fragrant evergreen herb with fine, green, fernlike foliage. Grows 3 to 10 inches high. Tiny, daisylike flowers. Spreads fast by creeping stems.

Light: Sun

Comments: Deep-rooted so resists drought. Used as lawn substitute where drought is extreme. Can be mowed, walked on. Tolerates partial shade. Plant divisions in early spring, 4 to 12 inches apart.

CREEPING PHLOX, MOSS PHLOX, GROUND PINK, MOSS PINK
Phlox subulata

Zone: 2–10

Description: Hardy, spreading plants 4 to 6 inches tall. Trailing stems make thick carpet of needlelike foliage. Pink, white, violet, or red flowers in early spring.

Light: Sun

Comments: A good choice for any well-drained soil. Desirable for brilliant color on slopes, edging perennial borders, cascading over walls, or in rock gardens. Rich soil not needed. Space plants 12 to 18 inches apart. After flowering, trim stems back halfway to stimulate new foliage. Easy to divide old plants for other areas.

CREEPING SPEEDWELL
Veronica repens

Zone: 5–10

Description: Shiny, dark green, ½- to ¾-inch, scalloped-edge leaves. Spreading mat is about 4 inches tall. Clusters of blue, pink, or white flowers in spring.

Light: Sun or light shade

Comments: Full sun in zones 5 to 8, light shade in 9 and 10. Grows best in moist soil enriched with organic matter. Space plants in early spring 6 to 12 inches apart. Plant in contained areas away from lawns.

CREEPING THYME
Thymus serpyllum

Zone: 3–10

Description: Hardy trailing, evergreen-forming, close-napped green carpet. Tiny ¼-inch leaves; fragrant flowers of red, pink, white, rosy purple in summer.

Light: Sun

Comments: Use between stepping-stones and as ground cover. Avoid rich soil; best in poor, dry, well-drained soil. It's hardy, tolerates neglect and traffic. Mow to keep plants in uniform shape and height. Space plants about 6 to 12 inches apart, and plant in spring. It's easy to divide old plants to start new ones in other areas.

EVERGREEN CANDYTUFT
Iveris sempervirens

Zone: 3

Description: Evergreen shrub grows 8 to 12 inches tall, with 24-inch spread. Dense, glistening, dark green, and cushiony. Roots in where stems touch soil. Two-inch white flower clusters in early spring, with some cultivars flowering at intervals all season.

Light: Sun

Comments: Handsome flower and foliage. Useful to cover ground or soften rocks in small areas. Needs well-drained soil containing organic matter. Adapts to seashore conditions. Space plants 12 to 18 inches apart or start from seed. Cut plants back part way after bloom.

FERNS, NEW YORK
Thelypteris noveboracensis

Zone: 2

Hay-scented
Dennstaedtia punctilobula

Zone: 3

Resurrection
Polypodium polypodioides

Zone: 7

Description: Long, gray-green fronds with paired, notched leaflets. Underside looks rusty.

Light: Shade

Comments: Many kinds of ferns, from 6 to 36 inches tall. They spread by root stalks underground.

Most ferns thrive best in moist soil high in leaf mold or peat. They add charm in natural settings or on the shady side of walls. Ferns die back in fall and reappear in spring. Space plants about 12 inches apart in an area with light shade; space larger ferns up to 18 inches apart.

FORGET-ME-NOT
Myosotis scorpioides 'semperflorens'

Zone: 5–10

Description: Narrow, 1- to 2-inch leaves. Pale blue ¼-inch flowers with pink, yellow, or white centers in spring and summer. Creeping stems grow dense quickly. Dies back in winter; reappears in spring.

Light: Shade

Comments: Grow in moist spots with light shade. Charming in natural setting. Needs rich, moist soil. Easy care and self-seeding. Plant 12 inches apart in early spring. Start new plants by dividing old ones.

GAZANIA, TRAILING

Gazania ringens 'leucolaena'

Zone: 8–10

Description: Creeping plant with 3- to 6-inch narrow leaves. Has 1½- to 2½-inch yellow, daisylike flowers in spring, with scattered flowers rest of season. Flowers love sun, but close on cloudy days. Runners will root as they grow out.

Light: Sun

Comments: Trailing habit makes it suitable to cover banks or cascade over walls, but it can cover flat spots. Plants resist drought, but water during extended heat. Tolerates poor soil. Space 18 to 24 inches apart. Discard old, woody plants every fourth year and use younger plants from divisions for replanting in early spring. Mulch.

INDIAN STRAWBERRY, MOCK STRAWBERRY

Duchesnea indica

Zone: 5–10

Description: Plant mat 2 to 3 inches thick. Has 3-leaflet, 1- to 3-inch leaves, similar to wild strawberry. Flowers are yellow, about ¾ inch across, followed by ½-inch red berries. Fruit is not tasty. Plant is semievergreen.

Light: Sun or shade

Comments: Runners shoot out quickly and root well for attractive cover in large areas. Avoid small areas. Thrives in any soil, including shaded areas on seashore or desert. Start from seed, or divide old plants in early spring or fall. Space plants 12 to 18 inches apart. Use leftover plants in hanging baskets.

LAMB'S-EARS, BETONY

Stachys byzantina

Zone: 3–10

Description: Soft, silvery, woolly-looking 4- to 6-inch leaves. Plant grows 12 to 18 inches tall. Spreads by underground roots to make solid mat of cover. Purplish flower spikes in summer. Generally grown for attractive leaves.

Light: Sun

Comments: Hardy in hot, well-drained, sunny areas. Space plants 12 to 18 inches apart. Needs little water. Grow from seed in spring or divisions of old plants in spring or

Lamium in flower

fall. Remove old foliage in spring. Feed lightly; water.

LAMIUM

Lamium sp.

Zone: 4–9

Description: Vigorous and fast-growing, 9 to 12 inches tall, with variegated, crinkled leaves and flowers in white, pink, lavender, and purple-red.

Light: Tolerates shade

Comments: It can get weedy or take over; contain it with edgings. Also called spotted dead nettle and yellow archangel. The word dead in the common name means this plant does not sting like a true nettle.

LANTANA, TRAILING

Lantana montevidensis

Zone: 9–10

Description: Evergreen, a trailing shrub in warm climates. Arching 18- to 24-inch-high canes covered with dark green, 1-inch-long, serrated leaves. Many fragrant ¾- to 1-inch clusters of lavender flowers. New varieties have white, yellow, and orange blooms.

Light: Sun

Comments: Makes colorful cover on sun-drenched slopes. Withstands drought and does best with occasional watering. Likes almost any soil. Root early fall cuttings and set out in spring. Space 18 inches apart. Also can be propagated by layering. Cut back plants before new growth in spring to eliminate old wood and stimulate thick branching and good flowering.

MAIDEN PINK, GARDEN PINK

Dianthus sp.

Zone: 2–10

Description: Forms dense, evergreen carpet of gray-green, grasslike leaves. Red, pink, or white, spicy smelling, ¾-inch-diameter flowers grow to 8 inches in late spring.

Light: Sun

Comments: Effective heavy-blooming cover for small areas and full sun. Fine for rock gardens. Keep well weeded until moderate spread fills bare ground. If weedy, difficult to seed later. Space 6 to 8 inches apart. Shear back lightly after flowering. Start new plants by dividing old ones or by root cuttings.

MOSS SANDWORT, IRISH MOSS, LAZY-MAN'S LAWN

Arenaria verna

Zone: 2–10

Description: Can be mistaken for moss when not in bloom. Forms 1- to 2-inch-high needlelike green foliage. White, ⅛-inch flowers above mat. Creeping runners spread fast, slightly mounding appearance.

Light: Sun or light shade

Comments: Useful for slopes and between stepping-stones. Needs light shade, well-drained soil. Divide existing plants in early spring; space 6 inches apart.

PACHYSANDRA, JAPANESE SPURGE

Pachysandra terminalis

Zone: 4–9

Description: Lush carpet 6 to 8 inches tall. Attractive leaves saw-toothed at edges. Evergreen. White flower heads above foliage in spring. Inconspicuous white berries may appear later.

Light: Shade

Comments: One of the most attractive and widely grown covers on level ground or slopes, in light to deep shade. Spreads slowly. Useful in beds, borders, dense shade under trees, and narrow spaces. Prefers moist, rich soil. Feed occasionally under trees or where there is root competition. Needs little care. Space plants 6 to 12 inches apart in spring. Start new plants from cuttings or divisions. Mulch young plants. Few weeds can grow in dense, established foliage.

PERIWINKLE, CREEPING MYRTLE, COMMON PERIWINKLE
Vinca minor

Zone: 4–7

Description: Fine, evergreen trailing carpet that roots in as it grows. About 6 inches high, glossy, ¾ to 1-inch leaves. Dotted with 1-inch-diameter, lavender-blue flowers in early spring.

Light: Sun or shade

Comments: Full sun in zones 4–7; light to deep shade in all areas. One of the best cover plants. Does well in most soils. Good for slopes. Little care except trimming once established. Start from cuttings or divisions. Space plants 12 to 18 inches apart. Makes nice backdrop for spring bulbs.

SILVER MOUND ARTEMISIA, SATINY WORMWOOD
Artemisia schmidtiana 'nana'

Zone: 3–10

Description: Produces attractive mound of silver-gray, finely cut foliage 1 foot tall. Tiny yellow flowers in late summer and early fall. Fast growth, cover forms quickly.

Light: Sun

Comments: Unusual foliage makes excellent accent. Likes any well-drained soil, needs little care, and resists drought. Space 12 to 15 inches apart in spring. Cut back to renew plant's mound shape.

SNOW-IN-SUMMER
Cerastium tomentosum

Zone: 2–10

Description: Grows 3 to 6 inches tall; produces tiny, fuzzy silvery-gray leaves. Many ½-inch, white flowers in early summer. Plant grows to 24 inches, with 48-inch spread. Self-sowing.

Light: Sun

Showy snow-in-summer

Comments: Does well in any well-drained soil, in desert, mountain, or coastal areas. Creeping stems spread quickly; makes hardy cover for large area. Grow between rocks. Space plants 12 to 24 inches apart. Start new plants by dividing old plants, seeds, or cuttings. When plants get scraggly, cut back to refresh appearance.

SPREADING ENGLISH YEW
Taxus baccata 'repandens'

Zone: 5–10

Description: Dwarf Japanese form grows about 3 inches tall, with long, trailing stems from base. Evergreen, needlelike foliage.

Light: Sun or shade

Comments: Best in rich, moist, well-drained soil. Space plants 36 to 48 inches apart in spring. Mulch between plants and grow annual flowers between yews until stems fill in spaces.

STONECROP SEDUM
Sedum sp.

Zone: 3–10

Description: Shallow-rooted, creeping runners spread fast. Many species are 2 to 3 inches high. Thick, fleshy, evergreen or semievergreen foliage. Shape, size, and color vary. Popular album species has ¼-inch evergreen leaves, reddish tips in winter.

Light: Sun or light shade

Comments: Useful between rocks, in stony areas, and on difficult slopes or banks. Moss stonecrop is weedy; it can cover an acre quickly with masses of yellow blossoms. Sedums will grow on poor soil and will resist drought and neglect. Needs only a light cover of leaves in winter. Space plants 9 to 12 inches apart. Divide old plants for new ones. For small area, Dragon's Blood is a newer cultivar with rich red color.

SWEET WOODRUFF
Galium odoratum

Zone: 4–10

Description: Distinctive because of 8 or 9 narrow, pointed leaves arranged like spokes on a wheel on square stems. Grows 6 to 8 inches tall. Leaves are fragrant. Clusters of tiny white flowers in spring and early summer.

Light: Shade

Comments: Useful beneath rhododendrons and high-branched conifer trees. Best in moist, acid, humus-rich soil. Space plants 10 to 12 inches apart. Divide in early spring or fall or start from seed.

THRIFT, SEA PINK, COMMON THRIFT
Ameria martima

Zone: 2–10

Description: Grasslike evergreen, about 6 inches tall, with narrow leaves. During spring and summer in cool areas, 10-inch flower stems bear ¾-inch clusters of white, pink, rose, or lilac flowers. Intermittent blooms in warm zones.

Light: Sun

Comments: Billowing cover in rock gardens or beds. Does well in sandy soil, near seashore, or in nearly any well-drained soil in full sun. Division of one large clump yields hundreds of new starts. Space 8 to 12 inches apart in early spring or fall. Mulch. For best show, lift, divide, and replant when centers of plants die. Use slow-release fertilizer in spring and fall.

WILD STRAWBERRY, SAND STRAWBERRY
Fragaria chiloensis

Zone: 3–10

Description: Plants spread quickly by runners for a shiny cover, 6 to 12 inches thick. Dark green leaves are 2 to 3 inches long. Many 1-inch white blossoms appear in spring, followed by red berries.

Light: Sun or light shade

Comments: Attractive cover that yields edible fruit. Shallow root system needs moisture. Space plants 12 to 18 inches apart. Remove blooms on new plants to produce runners. In early spring, set mower at 2-inch cutting height and mow off old foliage. Use a balanced fertilizer.

Zone Map

The key to successful gardening is knowing what plants are best suited for your area and when to plant them. This is true for every type of gardening. Climate maps, such as the one opposite, give a good idea temperature extremes by zones. By choosing plants best adapted to the different zones, and by planting them at the right time, you will have many more successes.

The climate in your area is a mixture of many different weather patterns, sun, snow, rain, wind, and humidity. To be a good gardener, you should know, on an average, how cold the garden gets in winter, how much rainfall it receives each year, and how hot or dry it becomes in a typical summer. You can obtain this general information from your state agricultural school or your county extension agent. In addition, acquaint yourself with the miniclimates in your own neighborhood, based on such factors as wind protection gained from a nearby hill, or humidity and cooling offered by a local lake or river. Then carry the research further by studying the microclimates that characterize your own plot of ground.

Here are a few points to keep in mind:

■ Plants react to exposure. Southern and western exposures are sunnier and warmer than northern or eastern ones. Light conditions vary greatly even in a small yard. Match your plants' needs to the correct exposure.

■ Wind can damage many plants, by either drying the soil or knocking over fragile growth. Protect plants from both summer and winter winds to increase their odds of survival and to save yourself the time and energy of staking plants and watering more frequently.

■ Consider elevation, too, when selecting plants. Cold air sweeps down hills and rests in low areas. These frost pockets are fine for some plantings, deadly for others. Plant vegetation that prefers a warmer environment on the tops or sides of hills, never at the bottom.

■ Use fences, the sides of buildings, shrubs, and trees to your advantage. Watch the play of shadows, the sweep of winds, and the flow of snowdrifts in winter. These varying situations are ideal for some plants, harmful to others. In short, always look for ways to make the most of everything your yard has to offer.

THE USDA PLANT HARDINESS MAP
OF THE UNITED STATES AND CANADA

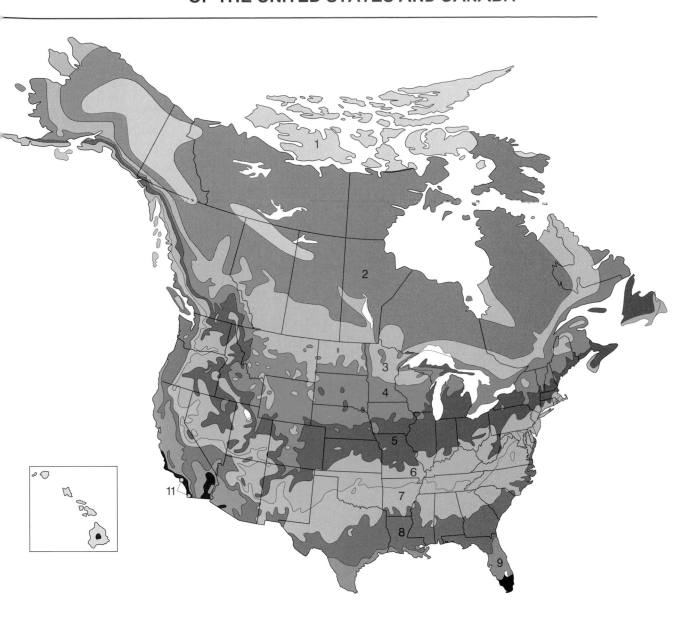

RANGE OF AVERAGE ANNUAL MINIMUM
TEMPERATURES FOR EACH ZONE

	ZONE 1	BELOW -50° F
	ZONE 2	-50° TO -40°
	ZONE 3	-40° TO -30°
	ZONE 4	-30° TO -20°
	ZONE 5	-20° TO -10°
	ZONE 6	-10° TO 0°
	ZONE 7	0° TO 10°
	ZONE 8	10° TO 20°
	ZONE 9	20° TO 30°
	ZONE 10	30° TO 40°
	ZONE 11	ABOVE 40°

Index